Riddle Rhymes

Charles Ghigna   Illustrated by Julia Gorton

HYPERION BOOKS FOR CHILDREN
NEW YORK

YOUR SECRET COMPANION

I follow you outside each day.
We share the morning sun.
I walk each time you take a step.
I run each time you run.

I go or stop each time you move.
I do just what you do.
I wear a suit of solid black.
My shape is just like you.

But as the sun begins to set
I slowly fade away.
I disappear into the night,
Yet reappear each day.

You'll find me lying on the ground
Right in front of you.
So wave hello to the one you know —
Your SHADOW — how do you do?

A GUEST IN THE GARDEN

I like flowers.
I like sun.
I like gardens
Just for fun.

I keep quiet
When I play.
I like praying
Every day.

I'm a slender,
Cautious creature.
I look like a
Tiny preacher.

I'm so still
And out of sight;
A PRAYING MANTIS —
Yes, that's right.

THE EVERLASTING LIGHT

I shine forever free.
I do not cost a cent.
I need no bulb or battery.
My light is permanent.

You'll find me way up in the sky,
When each new day's begun.
But do not look me in the eye —
I am the shining SUN.

THE INVISIBLE FRIEND

I ride the sky
And touch the ground.
I come and go
With just a sound.

Day or night
I live outside.
You can't see me,
But I don't hide.

I lift up kites.
I blow through trees.
I sail the boats.
I stir the leaves.

I'm not a ghost.
I'm just a friend.
Here I come —
I am the WIND.

THE SHINY-FACED FRIEND

You'll find me hanging on the wall
Looking back at you.
My shiny face is everyplace
For anyone to view.

You see me when you brush your teeth
And when you comb your hair.
I try to look just like you do.
Forgive me when I stare.

A wicked witch once asked of me,
"Who's the fairest of us all?"
But I, of course, could never say —
I'm just a MIRROR on the wall.

THE POLITE POINTER

I live high
Out on the farm.
I am found
Up on the barn.

A horse, a ship,
Or silent bird,
I point the way
Without a word.

I point East.
I point West.
I turn and turn
And never rest.

I show the way
In wind and rain.
That's why I'm called
A WEATHER VANE.

THE BRIGHTEST BOW

I wear a multicolored coat
Of ribbons framed in blue.
It shines each time that I come out
To bring good luck to you.

I hide until the rain is gone
And storm clouds disappear.
That's when I bend across the sky
To show that all is clear.

So next time when the rain clouds go,
Come find me way up high.
I am the one out in the sun,
A RAINBOW in the sky.

HIGH FLYER

I fly above the tallest trees.
I'm not a bird or plane.
I have no wings or feathered things.
I do not like the rain.

I play among the passing clouds.
I like to rise and sail.
I am a friend who loves the wind.
I'm big and have a tail.

I like the gusty month of March.
I soar way out of sight.
My shape is like a diamond.
I am a brand-new KITE.

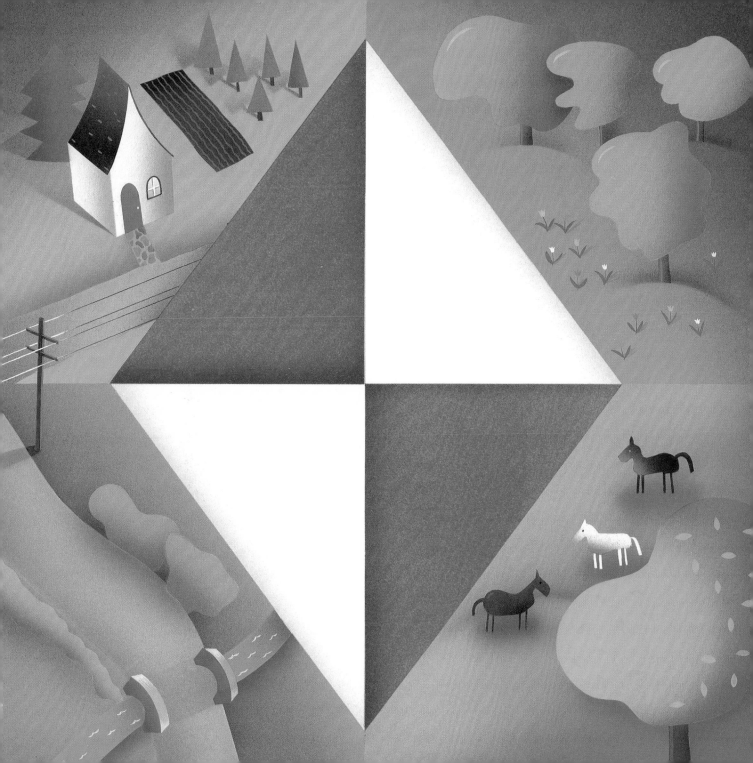

YOUR HIGHNESS

I am a free and open field
That's never out of bounds,
Where kites and planes and boomerangs
Can do their ups and downs.

I am the biggest yard of all,
Where birds begin their play
Of hide-n-seek among the clouds
At each new break of day.

I am the place called outer space,
Where nothing is too high.
I am the home of all the stars —
I am the endless SKY.

PARTY PAL

I'm bigger than a basketball.
I'm light and rather round.
I string along at party time.
I'm Happy Birthday bound.

I'm soft and plump and playful.
I'm slick and rather wide.
And when you sneeze or there's a breeze,
I like to take a ride.

I float and bob above your head.
I'm like a sailing moon.
I'm bursting to bring happiness —
That's me — a big BALLOON.

THE LONELY ROOM

From kitchen to the living room,
From bedroom to the bath,
I am the room you're passing through
No matter what your path.

You rarely stop to visit me
Except to sweep or dust;
Yet on the way to other rooms
I really am a must.

I am a narrow passage.
I lead the way for all.
I am a little, lonely room —
The one known as the HALL.

I have two hands.
I have a face.
I'm found in almost
Every place.

In the kitchen,
In the hall,
I like to hang
Upon the wall.

I like to sit
Beside your bed
Or on the shelf
Near books you've read.

I like to wake
You up each day
And send you off
To school or play.

I like to tick.
I like to tock.
Your timely friend—
I am a CLOCK.

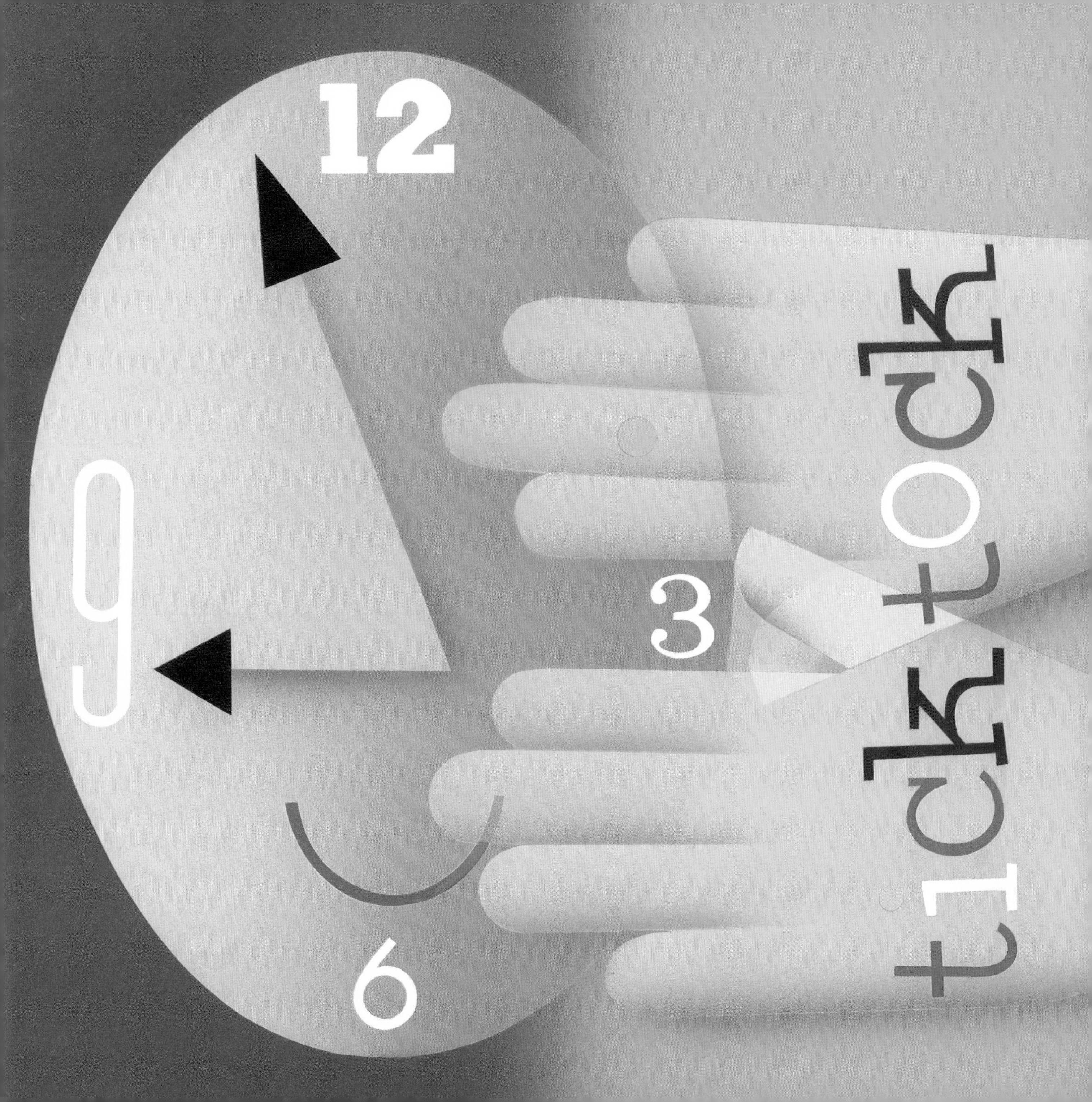
12
3
6
tick tock

UNDERCOVER FRIEND

Here I sit
Upon the shelf.
I'm not a toy.
I'm not an elf.

Yet I can take
You far away
To any place,
Night or day.

We'll travel to
Each foreign land,
Yet I will stay
Right in your hand.

My friends and I,
You will see,
Are full of facts
And fantasy.

So pick me up
And take a look.
Now you know —
I am a BOOK.

OCTOBER'S COLORFUL FRIENDS

I like sunshine.
I like trees.
I like dancing
With the breeze.

I turn orange.
I turn brown.
I go sailing
To the ground.

I am crispy.
I can crunch.
I get raked up
In a bunch.

I get stuffed
In scarecrow sleeves.
My friends and I
Are AUTUMN LEAVES.

YOUR FEATHERED FRIEND

Who?

All right! All right!
It's the middle of the night!
And I keep asking, "Who?"

To end this game
Just guess my name,
And then we'll both be through.

You'll find me perched
Up in a tree.
They say I'm wise and true.

Your friend, the fowl,
I'm Mister OWL—
Now you know who's WHOOO!

WHO

WHO

WHO

WHO

To my son Chip, who likes to rhyme
His words and riddles all the time
—C.G.

To my son Russell, he's number three,
I wonder who he'll turn out to be
—J.G.

FIRST EDITION

1   3   5   7   9   10   8   6   4   2

Library of Congress Cataloging-in-Publication Data

Ghigna, Charles.
Riddle rhymes/Charles Ghigna: illustrated by Julia Gorton— 1st ed.
p.   cm.
Presents a collection of fifteen "Who Am I?" and "What Am I?" rhyming riddles.
ISBN 1-56282-479-1 (trade)—ISBN 1-56282-480-5 (lib. bdg.)
1. Riddles, Juvenile.   2. Children's poetry.   [1. Riddles.   2. American poetry.]   I. Gorton, Julia, ill.   II. Title.
PN6371.5.G47   1995
818'.5402—dc20
94-18205
CIP
AC

The artwork for each picture is prepared using airbrushed acrylic on paper.
This book is set in 14-point Spartan Book.

Designed by Julia Gorton.

A C K N O W L E D G M E N T S

A number of these poems first appeared in the magazines listed below. The author wishes to thank the publishers and editors of
those publications for their permission to include them here. Some of the poems have been retitled and revised since their first
publication, and all poems are copyright Charles Ghigna.
"October's Colorful Friends," published as "A Fall Of Colors," *Turtle*, Oct. 1991.
"The Polite Pointer," *Lollipops*, Jan. 1991.
"Your Highness," published as "The Sky," *Child Life*, Feb. 1988.
"The Brightest Bow," *Humpty Dumpty*, Apr. 1993.
"A Guest in the Garden," *Lollipops*, Mar. 1991.
"A Timely Friend," published as "The Clock Song," *Lollipops*, Jan. 1990.
"Your Feathered Friend," published as "Who Done It?" *Lollipops*, Sept. 1990.